The In Crowd

DEALING WITH PEER PRESSURE

by Amy Rechner

Content Adviser:
Billy AraJeJe Woods, Ph.D.,
Department of Psychology, Saddleback College,
Mission Viejo, California

Reading Adviser:
Alexa L. Sandmann, Ed.D.,
Professor of Literacy, College and Graduate School
of Education, Health, and Human Services,
Kent State University

Compass Point Books
151 Good Counsel Drive
P.O. Box 669
Mankato, MN 56002-0669

This book was manufactured with paper containing at least 10 percent post-consumer waste.

Photographs ©: Capstone Press/Karon Dubke, cover; Alamy/PHOTOTAKE Inc., 5, Wendy White, 7, ACE STOCK LIMITED, 9, 16, Nancy Honey, 24, Bubbles Photolibrary, 37; PhotoEdit Inc./David Young-Wolff, 10; 123RF/ Mandy Godbehear, 12; Newscom, 13, 30; Shutterstock/Gina Smith, 17, PHOTOCREO Michal Bednarek, 25, Jaimie Duplass, 31, Yuri Arcurs, 33; Corbis/Richard Wright, 21, Hill Street Studios/Stock This Way, 28, Nathan Benn, 35, Keystone/Martin Ruetschi, 39; fotolia/Galina Barskaya, 27, moodboard, 40; Getty Images Inc./Taxi/Chris Clinton, 42.

For Compass Point Books
Brenda Haugen, Ashlee Suker, Jo Miller, LuAnn Ascheman-Adams, Joe Ewest, Nick Healy, and Catherine Neitge

For Bow Publications
Bonnie Szumski, Kim Turner, and Katy Harlowe

Library of Congress Cataloging-in-Publication Data
Rechner, Amy.
  The in crowd : dealing with peer pressure / by Amy Rechner.
    p. cm. — (What's the Issue?)
  Includes index.
  ISBN 978-0-7565-1891-2 (library binding)
1. Peer pressure in adolescence—Juvenile literature. 2. Teenagers—Life skills guides—Juvenile literature. 3. Conformity—Juvenile literature. 4. Peer pressure—Juvenile literature. I. Title.
  HQ799.2.P44R43 2009
  303.3'270835—dc22   2008039482

Visit Compass Point Books on the Internet at *www.compasspointbooks.com* or e-mail your request to *custserv@compasspointbooks.com*

TABLE OF CONTENTS

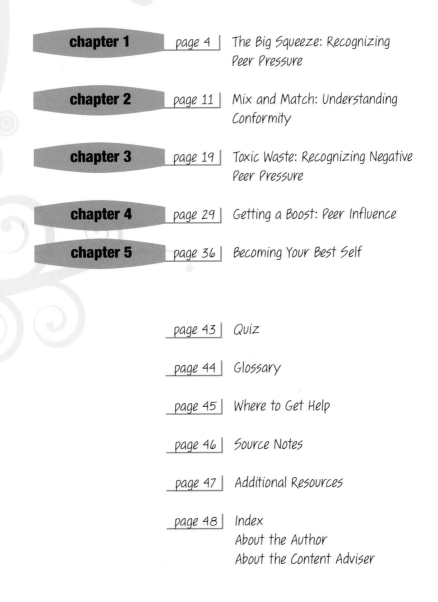

CHAPTER one

THE BIG SQUEEZE: RECOGNIZING PEER PRESSURE

How old were you when you first encountered peer pressure? Ten? Eleven? Try this—you were probably around 4, if not younger.

Peer pressure, the influence that friends and classmates have on each other's behavior, begins almost the same day a child starts playing with other children. A fan of *Dora the Explorer* pretends she prefers *SpongeBob SquarePants* because her friend does. A timid swimmer tries harder so he can join his friends in the pool. The desire to fit in with a group is basic. People crave acceptance the same way many crave french fries.

Stephanie* remembers feeling pressured to fit in even when she was much younger. "There's always a minor version of peer pressure, even in preschool," she said. "I knew even then that if I didn't want to play in the sandbox or didn't want to draw with markers when others did, they'd

* This and other names in this book have been changed for privacy reasons.

leave me alone, which I didn't want. I'd do what everyone else did, or I'd be left by myself. It just gets stronger when you get older."

While peer pressure is always around—even Dr. Seuss' Sam-I-Am used peer pressure to push green eggs and ham—it starts getting really intense in middle school. You're growing up, maturing in all kinds of uncomfortable ways, and your relationship with your parents is changing. You need your space.

Make New Friends, Keep the Old?

When kids enter adolescence, it's entirely normal for them to look outside of their families for support, guidance, and advice. The parents who

knew everything for the first 12 years are suddenly uncool, while friends, classmates, and even enemies understand your questions and appear to know the answers. It's at this point that your peer group becomes a

Peer pressure can lead you to do things you shouldn't.

major influence.

"The students who struggle academically and who don't have strong social skills are the most likely to get sucked in by peer pressure," noted a school social worker. "They think, 'Oh my gosh, this cool kid is talking to me. If I do whatever he or she says I'll be in this group.' Kids are looking for acceptance. They want to be part of something."

Erin remembers how peer pressure affected friendships in her middle school and high school years. "There would be

"Girls would gang up and say things like, 'Don't talk to this person. You're friends with us.'"

a lot of politics within groups of friends," she recalled. "Girls would gang up and say things like, 'Don't talk to this person. You're friends with us.' There was always changing in the group. One day someone would decide 'we hate this girl,' and that meant I was supposed to hate her, too."

Sometimes peer pressure

Hang in There!

Going into his sophomore year, Mike recalls middle school as a time when kids were forced to learn social skills as they met new classmates. "All the kids were snotty. I was one of them," he said. "In the hallways, girls would always be making fun of each other, and they were brutal. The guys weren't much better." Some kids dealt with the social pressure by not dealing with it, choosing instead to be out-siders. The ones who struggled, Mike noted, eventually found their place. "No one is at the bottom social level forever. Try to make new friends, and things will change." He said high school is easier. "It's such a big place is pretty obvious, like being persuaded to shoplift or to turn against another student. Other times it can happen without you even realizing it. It's not always bad, either.

Test your peer pressure IQ: Which of these examples could be called peer pressure?

- A friend urges you to try sushi, and even though you think it looks like bait, you do. Surprise! You like it!
- Your mom says no unsupervised boy-girl activities are allowed, but when you're invited to join a friend with a mixed group at the movies you go rather than be left out.
- The pop quiz on the abolition of slavery is easy, but your friend looks stumped. Poor guy!

He must have spaced out during yesterday's discussion. He gives you a desperate look, so you move your paper on the desk to make your answers easy to see.

If you said all of these scenarios are examples of peer pressure, you're right. In each case, you were influenced to do something you probably wouldn't have done on your own. Of course,

You know that letting a friend copy your work is wrong—even if he is captain of the football team.

A Force of Nature

In any group of friends, there will always be one or two who are interested in romance before the rest of the group. Pressure to date is often the first organized pressure guys and girls face. How do they deal with it?

- "My friends pressured me into asking out this one girl. It felt like I had to do this. I kind of wanted to, I was thinking about it, but it was almost like they forced me to do it. Fortunately, she said yes."
  —Mike

- "There was a guy in my group and my friends were telling me he really liked me. I didn't really know him, but figured I should see what he was like. He turned into kind of a jerk, and I didn't really like him. Finally, things fizzled off."
  —Elise

- "There's always pressure to hook up with your girlfriend, or just any girl. People always made a big deal about this. I mean everybody."
  —Rob

- "There was always that group of girls that did sexual stuff. They were known for that, and they stayed with that, until they had a chance to reinvent themselves in high school."
  —Erin

there's no law against giving sushi to minors, but hey, pressure is pressure.

Can You Hear Me Now?

Peer pressure is often seen as pressure to join a clique or to do bad things, but there's much more to it than that. Look at what you're wearing today. Peer pressure probably had something to do with why you bought those clothes in the first place. Did you do your homework yesterday? Peer pressure may have influenced that, too. Did you ignore somebody you don't like? Peer pressure again.

It's difficult to resist when someone tries to talk you into something. What you may not realize is that people often persuade you without using any words at all. Unspoken peer pressure

Most teens want to blend in. They dress like their friends and buy the same gadgets.

is very powerful—when you see how others dress or act, you know you're supposed to do the same thing. The pressure to conform is simply enormous during the teen years.

"The earliest example of peer pressure I can remember is to buy clothes from Hollister, Abercrombie, and other expensive stores, because all of the popular people were shopping there," Lauren said.

Even if you don't follow the popular kids, other people's opinions still matter, she noted. "What your friends like can be the greatest influence for that kind of thing." No one has to say a word to you about it. You know what you're supposed to wear just by looking around.

While pressure to dress like everyone else is the most obvious kind of unspoken peer pressure, it's not the only kind. Unspoken pressure can also be a really positive force in your life, especially make it, too. If doing well is important to your friends, it will also be important to you.

Oh, Grow Up

Peer pressure doesn't go away as you become an adult. It crops up whenever people talk about politics or money or material things. There are adult Mean Girls still playing their power games (how pathetic is that?!). For most people, peer pressure becomes much less important as you get older. Learning to deal with peer pressure now will make it much easier to stand up to pressure you feel is unhealthy or just plain stupid

Peer pressure can affect the stores you choose.

when you're out on your own. You don't want to be an adult who feels like a loser for driving the "wrong" car, or who spends so much on trendy clothes that you can hardly afford food, or who hurts other people's feelings. You're way better than that.

if it motivates you to do your best at something. You may push yourself to try harder at soccer if your friend is determined to bend it like Beckham and you share his interest. Another friend headed for the honor roll can motivate you to study so you can

CHAPTER two

MIX AND MATCH: UNDERSTANDING CONFORMITY

Let's talk about conformity, the desire to fit in with everyone else. First of all, it is important to understand that there is absolutely nothing wrong with wanting to fit in. It is human. When you were a little kid, your parents did your conforming for you. They signed you up for gymnastics or T-ball. They took you to see *Shrek* or *Finding Nemo* so you'd be able to talk about them with other kids. Maybe they even bought you an American Girl doll or a Nintendo so your toys would fit in, too.

As you've grown, you've made a lot of choices based on the desire to conform, probably without realizing it—your clothes, your hairstyle, what sports you like. Again, this is totally normal. Kids learn pretty early that being different can sometimes hurt.

Would you stand up to the crowd when they're making fun of a friend's new glasses?

Square Peg, Meet Round Hole

Once you hit the teen years, though, the pressure to conform becomes more intense than it's ever been before. Suddenly a simple choice—such as the shirt you're wearing—is seen as a symbol of your willingness to fit in. Never mind that you chose that shirt because it was the only clean one you had. In a group's shared brain, it defines who you are and whether you're in or out. It's at this point that you may need to decide how important to you "belonging" is and how much conforming you want to do.

"As you mature you develop different ways of understanding the world," said one expert. "Starting in middle school kids are all changing, and that makes everything even more confusing. Peers start dividing into groups, and you have more time on your own. Your task is to figure out what group you belong to."

Going up a grade and leaving a familiar school for a new, larger one with lots of new classmates can be a rough transition for groups of friends. Everyone is growing at different rates, and interests change, especially as kids meet new people. One day you and your best friend are playing a favorite game together. The next day he's gone off with new friends who share his interest in girls, leaving you on your own. The time has come to find some new friends.

This creates a tricky situation for many adolescents. Not only

If your friend becomes more interested in girls while you're more interested in sports, maybe it's time to find some new friends who share your interests.

are they under greater pressure to conform, but they also need to figure out exactly which group suits them. At the same time, they look in the mirror and barely recognize their reflections. Relationships with family and old friends change. New experiences and interests fill their heads. That's a lot to deal with, plus the fear of being alone and friendless. It's no surprise that people are more susceptible to pressure to conform for the sake of new friends.

Stephanie never made conforming a priority, even though she knew the risks. "When you don't conform as a kid you may be lonely sometimes, but you don't worry about it ruining your life. When you get older you think being isolated is almost life threatening, socially."

Julia recalled a situation from middle school where a friend's resentment of Julia's new social status created an ugly situation.

"She had been my best friend, but the friendship ended because I felt like she was using me for homework. When I started hanging out with a sports crowd, she wanted to be in that group, too, but she didn't play any sports. She started doing nasty things, pulling me into fights with other people."

Camouflage: Dressed for Battle

Elise said the greatest pressure she's faced in school is about appearance. "I worry about what I would wear, what would my friends think of me, would I look dorky," she said. "I want to impress my friends. I want to look cool." Watching her friends experiment with makeup or new fashions, Elise is sometimes tempted to follow their style examples, but she doesn't get carried away. "Sometimes I feel comfortable, other times I don't think I look right and just want

Peer Pressure and Homework

A recent high school graduate, Julia made a name for herself as a dedicated student. Her good grades made her a prime target for less motivated students. "As early as fifth grade everyone wanted to copy my homework. Friends would beg, and even though I knew it was wrong I would end up letting them." As she continued to pull A's through high school, the pressure continued. "There are some people who won't leave you alone. They'll just take your work if you leave it on your desk. Sometimes I'd lie to them and say I left it in my locker." Although she fought against sharing her work, classmates never stopped hassling her. Julia's hard work paid off when she was voted into the National Honor Society, but the cheaters weren't so lucky. "One girl took my paper and photocopied it. But she got caught because my name was on it."

to go home and change."

Clothes and hairstyles are pretty easy ways to fit in with the crowd. However, working too hard to fit in can go beyond fashion, sometimes leading people to abandon or hide hobbies and interests because new friends don't share them.

Sometimes the desperation to be part of a group can cause someone to suppress his or her own personality in order to fit in. Your new friends watch *American Idol*, so you do. They complain about their parents, so you do. They have long, sleek hair and wear flip-flops, so you invest in a hair straightener and pray for warm weather.

Bit by bit, the Real You is hidden behind the Pretend You—

that you're really a curly-haired, *Singin' in the Rain* lovin' teen with cold feet. All they see is a teen who looks like them and rolls her eyes when they do.

Unfortunately, that strategy can backfire.

Who Do You Think You Are?

When the year begins at a new school, many groups form naturally. The jocks, the popular girls, and the band kids all seem to find one another with minimal effort. For the rest of the student population, finding a place is much trickier. Those with a strong sense of self seek friends who

Wearing makeup is one way girls try to fit in.

the version that your friends will find acceptable. The fact that your favorite part of the week is watching old movies with your dad is a deep, dark secret. Your new friends don't know

share their interests, regardless of social status. Others, struggling to match their identity to their ambitions, often put their energy into trying to break into their "dream" clique. While they're

Do Your Friends Make You Look Fat?

A 2008 study states that how girls feel about their weight is determined by their peer group. The study, which focused on girls ages 13 to 18, looked at girls in various groups. The girls who identified themselves as "Jocks" were less concerned about their weight and need to diet than any other group. Girls who were part of the nonconformist "Alternatives" group or who identified with kids who were in frequent trouble ("Burnouts") placed a high premium on being thin. Girls who called themselves "Average" and were not part of any specific group were the most likely to be unhappy with their appearance and to try various methods of losing weight.

unaffiliated, they'll do whatever they can to belong. Experts note that these "floaters" or "wannabes" often feel little respect for themselves, so they readily give up their own personalities in favor of a more popular model. However, this tactic often leaves them with lower self-esteem than before

Teens often group one another into categories, such as the band kids or the jocks.

and doesn't always win them entry into their dream clique.

But what if it does? You changed your appearance, your habits, and your hobbies, and now you fit in with the group. Maybe you even gave up some old friends in the process because they weren't cool enough.

Erin found her close group of friends in middle school and stuck with them. However, she recalls seeing girls try to worm their way in to more popular groups and wondering why they bothered. "People would have to change to get into a group," she said. "You could always tell the posers."

The effect on self-esteem can be lasting, Erin observed. "You won't be sure of yourself growing up. You're always going to second-guess yourself. You're always going to think you have to conform," she said. "You're never going to have that confidence, and I think that's key to have. People can always tell if you're trying too hard. It's not that hard to spot a phony."

It's a lot of hard work to pretend to be someone you're not. It's also risky. Now that you've given up your old identity, everything hinges on this one working out. If people catch on that you're faking it, there's a real risk of being ostracized by

"You won't be sure of yourself growing up. You're always going to second-guess yourself. You're always going to think you have to conform."

both your new friends and your old ones. That leaves you with no one, which is what you were trying to avoid in the first place.

CHAPTER three

TOXIC WASTE: RECOGNIZING NEGATIVE PEER PRESSURE

By now you've realized that peer pressure is an invisible hand that tries to move you around like a chess piece. However, you are not a pawn. Nobody can make you do anything unless you choose to go along with him or her.

The choice to go along with a crowd isn't always a bad one. Few people suffer long-term damage from following fashion trends. However, there are many cases when caving in to pressure is a very bad idea, and you should be ready to say no and mean it.

The long, bumpy road to adulthood starts in middle school and continues through the high school years. It's an adventure and a time for new experiences. Some guys and girls are more adventuresome than others, and that's when the heat is on. More than once you will be challenged to choose between what you think is right and what your friends are doing. "Everyone matures differently, and as a young teen's identity develops, he struggles to find the norm," said Marc Atkins, an expert in adolescent psychology. "Kids are making quick decisions, and some make mistakes, withdrawing from friends because they're no longer cool."

While some peer pressure is obvious—someone calls you a loser or tells you everyone's doing "it"—unspoken pressure is much harder to deal with. How do you defend yourself against a dirty look or turned backs?

Rob had a tough time in middle school. "That's when the whole drug scene really came up," he recalled. "I remember kids asking me almost daily if I smoked or whatever. The first time I met a new kid they always asked." Pressure continued despite his refusal to join in.

A former teacher in an alternative high school notes that Rob's situation is not unusual. The students in her classroom frequently pressured each other to act out. "What kids need to realize is that there are alternatives," she said. "I always told my students, 'How can you be safe? How can you make a better choice?'"

Everybody's Doing It? Everybody Who?

While many kids feel they are the only ones resisting temptation, the truth is different. A survey of 12,000 middle and high school students in the Midwest shows that 78 percent don't smoke. More than 60 percent avoid being around drinking, and 80 percent reject marijuana use.

"Kids need to check out the norms, talk to their friends about what they do and think," said Atkins. "Don't assume that

Stop and think about the consequences of your actions before making a choice.

Stay Strong

Rob has a gift for poetry that he hides behind a tough facade. As a frequent new kid in school, he found easier acceptance among those on the fringes of school society— the ones who experimented with drugs, took to smoking at an early age, and other negative behaviors. He found an inner strength that kept him out of serious trouble. "I never did anything to put myself in the way of extreme harm or danger," he said. "I always analyze the situations I put myself into, even more when someone could get hurt." Now settled in high school in a new community, Rob has good advice for those interested in a walk on the wild side. "Just stop and think. Don't act, think."

everyone is doing something. You may find out that people are more like you."

Since everybody knows that you're not supposed to smoke,

drink, do drugs, cheat, steal, or be mean, why is it so easy to be talked into doing it? It's really quite simple. No one wants to be left out, labeled a dork, or otherwise rejected by a peer group. Besides, you're curious, tempted—and you can usually convince yourself that a little experiment once in awhile is no big deal.

Another reason is that you trust your friends. They've got your back, right? Unfortunately, when it comes to risky behavior,

21

no one wants to do it alone. Your friend just wants you at his side when he jumps off that cliff.

Erin's been there. "Friends will point out all the ways around getting in trouble, and they'd completely convince you that it's going to be OK," she said. "I think you have that devil on your shoulder, too, so when friends come up with a plan it's easy to go along with it."

"During the grade school years, parents are pretty influential in choosing friends," noted the high school teacher. "They need to train you to look out for the right qualities and remind you that it's OK not to trust people right away."

People often cave under pressure because they're afraid of being ostracized. Elise has seen it happen. "Sometimes the group won't forgive someone for not going along," she said. "It's sad, and it's hard to watch because they're not friends anymore. The kicked-out one would try to get back in the group, apologizing and saying she just didn't want to do that one thing."

Why Does Peer Pressure Work?

The adolescent brain isn't wired for caution.

- Teenagers in early adolescence are drawn to the immediate rewards of a potential choice and are less attentive to the possible risks.
- Teenagers in general are still learning to control their impulses, to think ahead, and to resist pressure from others.
- These skills develop gradually, and a teen's ability to control his or her behavior gets better throughout adolescence.

Standing Your Ground

Picture this: Everyone's meeting at a friend's house to go to

Risky Business

Peer pressure often leads teens into risky behaviors. Look at the trends in risky behaviors among high schoolers—look familiar?

- 11 percent of students surveyed rarely or never wore a seat belt when someone else was driving
- 18 percent carried a weapon
- 19.7 percent used marijuana
- 20 percent currently smoke cigarettes
- 29 percent rode in a car with a driver who had been drinking alcohol
- 44.7 percent currently drink alcohol
- 47.8 percent have had sexual intercourse

the high school football game together. You arrive to find that plans have changed—the parents are out of town. Next thing you know, some of the coolest kids on the planet walk in with some beer and a bag of Doritos. Music's on, cigarette smoke fills the air, and your buddy passes you a plastic cup. You know you will be grounded until you're 40 if you're caught smoking or drinking, and you don't really want to, except for the chance to hang out with the A-list kids. What do you do?

Use Your Good Manners

Say no, say thank you, and say good-bye. You don't have to explain why. No one really cares why you're not joining in, so don't work overtime to invent an excuse. Just "No thanks,"

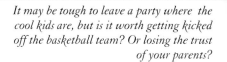

It may be tough to leave a party where the cool kids are, but is it worth getting kicked off the basketball team? Or losing the trust of your parents?

or "Sorry, can't" should do the trick, or at most, "I'm not in the mood." Then leave, since even being there is risky.

Reject the Behavior, Not the People

The evening has definitely turned into something you want no part of. However, these people are your friends, and

Lauren has a full calendar and a strong group of friends, but she's very aware of pressures to conform at her school. "There's a lot of pressure to be gorgeous, or to have a lot of boyfriends," she said. "The clique situation here is very noticeable, but a lot of girls mingle with the others." While Lauren hasn't strayed from her values, she's had friends who weren't so strong. "I make my own decisions. But I have a few friends who have been tempted into drinking alcohol and doing drugs because their 'more popular' friends wanted them to."

they're going along with it for reasons of their own. You don't need to make a big deal about their choices, especially at that particular moment. It's possible that you're not the only one there who doesn't want to join in. Check out how others feel about being there, and maybe you'll find someone you can leave with. Finding a buddy to leave the party with can make doing it easier. You can talk to your pals later about partying. If your refusal to join in becomes a deal-breaker, then these are not the friends for you. Move on, and be grateful for the buddy system—you know you're not truly alone, and it will make finding new friends easier.

Stephanie feels that her behavior is her responsibility, but what her friends do isn't. "There's a fine line between nagging about what your friends

If your friends are doing something you know is wrong or that makes you uncomfortable, don't be afraid to just walk away. You may find others are walking with you.

do and just doing what's right for yourself," she said.

Julia's decision not to drink has been repeatedly challenged by her classmates. She said, "I've never gone drinking, never been drunk. I've only gone to one party where there was alcohol, because my friend wanted to go and I went along to make sure she was all right. I was out of there by midnight, with my friend. The kids gave me grief about not drinking, and it was kind of scary. My friends say 'it would be the funniest thing to get Julia drunk and videotape it,' so I wouldn't even go to these parties."

Although it was hard to be the only one not drinking, Julia's confident she made the right choice. "Any picture where there's alcohol in it, and it's on the Internet, you can be kicked off your team, or suspended from school. It's just not worth it. Also, it's illegal, so why can't you wait?"

Call for Backup

In spite of your best efforts, sometimes the pressure just doesn't quit, and caving in starts to sound good. In the case of the impromptu beer party, if you're stuck without a ride, do not hesi-

Peer Pressure History: How Not to Play Ball

In 1919, Chicago White Sox first baseman Arnold Gandil pressured seven of his teammates into deliberately losing the World Series against Cincinnati in what became known as the "Black Sox Scandal." The players were caught and banned from major league baseball for life.

tate to call your parents and ask them to get you. If they're not available, call someone else—a neighbor, a grandparent, or anyone you trust who can pick you up. Seriously, adults are not going to be upset that you called and asked for help getting away from a bad situation.

"You really don't realize your parents are cool until late high school," Erin said. "Before then you think they're in a totally different realm. Kids need to stop being afraid of their parents. Don't underestimate them, and don't always think you're going to be grounded. They will tell you when you're doing the right thing. They've been in your shoes, and once you realize

Don't be afraid to call your parents if you need help.

that you'll be able to feel closer to them."

If the pressure you feel is so intense and ongoing that you feel unable to deal with it, the time has come to look for outside help. The school social worker

A trusted adult can be a great resource. He or she has probably experienced peer pressure and knows how to help you.

and counselors are trained to help adolescents with exactly this sort of thing. If you don't want to talk to someone at school, find an adult in your life whom you trust to help you come up with survival strategies—parents (yours or a friend's), other relatives or family friends, clergy, or a professional counselor or therapist.

Studies have shown that adolescents who have supportive relationships with their parents or other adults are less likely to be vulnerable to negative peer pressure. Make it your business to open lines of communication with a trustworthy adult. You'll enjoy it long after middle school and high school are over.

CHAPTER four

GETTING A BOOST: PEER INFLUENCE

We've talked a lot about peer pressure and how bad it can be. Peer pressure has an opposite, though—the much nicer peer influence. Peer influence is the good stuff—friends who set positive examples for each other or cheer each other on to excel or do good things.

Like its evil twin, peer pressure, peer influence depends largely on your friends. If you decide to reinvent yourself by making new friends with a group of thrill seekers, or you try to climb the social ladder to a more popular group, beware! You will probably encounter negative peer pressure, since you'll be outside your comfort zone and seeking guidance. On the other hand, if you choose to surround yourself with people who share your interests and treat you with respect, you will feel more secure. Good friends can have a positive influence on each other. Best of all, they serve as a line of protection against the negative influences that can seem so tempting.

Aim for the Middle

Look around the school cafeteria, and you'll see how all the groups are divided. Research shows that there are four basic kinds of groups in middle and high school culture:

1. The popular kids, who appear, from the outside view, to have the most friends, fun, and excitement.

2. The wannabes, who model themselves after the popular group.

3. Friendship circles—small groups of friends, each with their own mini-culture, often brought together through common interests such as online gaming, skateboarding, sports, etc.

Surrounding yourself with happy, positive people can help make you feel happy and positive, too.

4. Loners, who seem to have no friends and perhaps envy the kids who appear to fit in naturally.

It's easier to be yourself with a few really close friends.

While it might appear that the super-cool, A-list kids are the happiest, researchers found that it's better to be part of a smaller friendship circle. Individuals in these smaller groups generally feel good about themselves, researchers found. Without the pressure to keep up and be a certain way, members of these smaller groups have greater self-esteem and a healthier self-image. The best news? Happy people make better friends.

"It's so important to have positive influences in your life, especially during adolescence," a high school teacher said. "It's important for kids to remember that while it's wonderful to have a lot of friends, to have one true friend—that means everything."

As discussed earlier, you'll be safer from negative pressure if there's a strong adult in your life whom you can confide in and turn to for advice. Good friends can fill that function, too, especially if you have similar values. You may not feel comfortable talking to your mom about the pressure to fool around or hook up. However, your best friend will understand how you feel about it. She can help you make smart choices.

"The good kind of pressure happens with my friends and me as a group," said Stephanie. "We want to volunteer for the kindergartners, and I want some of my friends to do cross-country with me. I can tell I have influence with my friends, because after I became vegetarian some of them did, too."

Take the "A" Train

Having friends who exert a positive influence can make you smarter, too. The urge to conform can be a great motivator when your peer group is aiming for the honor roll.

"If a student gets into the right group, and that group has the intellectual ability to get the B's and A's, they try harder," noted a school social worker.

Mike finds his friends are great motivators to do well in school. "When the report cards come in, everyone's asking what your grades are," he said. "You don't want to walk away with C's and D's. I know my friends are getting straight B's, so I'm trying for A's and B's."

Strong Foundation

Erin understood early on how important it was to have friends in her corner, and she worked hard to keep them. "Even if you have just one person, and build on that, you'll be OK when you go into high school. You can build off that. You're not going to be alone. Plus, it will be easier for a group to approach a couple of you, instead of just one." She offers this advice for people whose friends are headed down a different path. "Find someone else. Conform in a good way. Try new things. Experimentation doesn't have to mean bad stuff. Go out for soccer. Get an after-school job. Find any excuse to try something new."

Studying with friends can be fun and help improve your grades.

Find Your Happy Place

Perhaps you're reading this and wondering how you can get some of that good peer influence when all of your friends from childhood seem to have disappeared. The breaking up of old friendships is one of the hardest things about adolescence. What's a shy-among-strangers person to do?

The best advice is also the most obvious: Find supervised activities that interest you at school or elsewhere and get involved. Not only will you meet like-minded people, you'll also fill your time with something more worthwhile than watching *Degrassi* reruns after school.

"The busier you are, the less stuff comes your way, and it helps you to stay away from unsupervised risks," a psychology expert noted. "If you work on your interests and relax a little bit about social status, the peer stuff can slide by a little."

Julia found most of her friends through sports and choir.

33

Best of Both Worlds

Elise spent her elementary school years in a Spanish-language immersion program. After five years with the same 30 kids, she went on to middle school, where the close-knit group began to break up. "I had to make new friends," she recalled. "It was a little hard at first, but I got to know the people in my classes and see them every day." Still Elise worked hard to maintain ties with her old friends, too. "There are times in the cafeteria when there's not an open spot at my friends' lunch table, so I'll have to go sit with another group. When that happens you never know if people are going to say hi or ignore you. My old friends from grade school are all in different cliques now, so I can sit with anyone and not feel weird."

When one group of friends fractured, she was able to find new friends through the other. "For most of middle school you're meeting new people. In high school it wasn't meeting new people, but hanging out with different groups of people."

Rob agrees that school clubs or activities can provide refuge. "I never felt much peer pressure in clubs or activities," he recalled. "Usually there was an adult there keeping us occupied, or we'd keep ourselves busy. There was never too much trouble there."

Running Interference

Of course, the best kind of peer influence is when your friends

"I never felt much peer pressure in clubs or activities."

prevent you from doing something you'll later regret. It's easy for your judgment to be clouded, especially if you're trying to get close to a particular person or group of people. Bad choices are often made when you're trying to impress someone.

"Peer pressure isn't always

Get involved! Joining the choir or a sports team are great ways to meet new friends.

negative," said Rob. "Maybe you're about to make a stupid decision and someone is there encouraging you not to."

Perhaps the object of your affection is a budding graffiti artist, or just a kid who likes spray paint. The idea of sneaking out after curfew to decorate a blank wall suddenly sounds glamorous and exciting. It will be your true friend who points out that not only is it illegal to do so, but it's also not really your thing and stupid, too. Friends can save you from yourself.

Lauren has been in that position as well. "Most of my friends claim that if I ever do drugs or start drinking, they will 'kill me' or 'beat my stupid butt,'" she said. "I guess you could call that positive!"

35

CHAPTER five

BECOMING YOUR BEST SELF

When pressure to be or act a certain way starts to build, the first piece of advice out of an adult's mouth is often, "Just be yourself." That can be pretty annoying, since the whole point of adolescence is trying to figure out who you are.

There's lots of information coming at you that tells you what you should like—which fashion labels, which energy drink, which TV show, which music, which superhero.

As you've seen, peer pressure can be a pretty big part of your life, if you let it. It's hard to separate your own likes and dislikes from those around you, but it's also the way to start becoming the person you want to be. This may seem hard to believe, but some teens don't like chocolate. If you don't like chocolate, then go ahead and don't like it. If someone offers you a candy bar, be the guy who doesn't like chocolate, instead of the guy who pretends he does and has to choke down a Hershey bar. That may seem like a pretty minor thing, but every time you declare your own like or dislike, you claim a little more power for the Real You.

Once you commit to being the authentic version of yourself, instead of the image you're being sold by other kids, TV, the Internet, or whatever, then put your energy into making it happen. Imagine that you're a jigsaw puzzle— the bajillion pieces that make up the Whole Authentic You include friends, peers, parents, teachers, the seriously cute high school senior across the street, Jamba Juice, and anyone or anything else that occupies some of your head space. You get to decide who or what is a

Teens spend a lot of time trying to figure out who they are. Don't let others decide for you.

piece of your puzzle by choosing the influences in your life. Choose wisely.

Words of Wisdom From a Panel of Peers

Rob: "What you do now will mold and shape your future in a big way. If you feel like you have no power now, trust me—you have a ton."

Elise: "If you know it's wrong, don't do it. Don't take the easy way out by following what your friends are doing."

Lauren: "Be strong, and be able to stand up for what you think is right, and don't let other people's opinions change the way you think."

Stephanie: "If you are yourself and don't try to be anybody else people will accept you. To get people interested in you, be interested in them first."

Mike: "Show confidence. If people see your confidence they'll want to talk to you more."

Julia: "I know everyone says this, but you have to think about what you're doing. Think before you speak; think before you do. If people are going to criticize you for not doing something, they're not really your friends. You really have to ignore it and just keep being a good kid."

Erin: "Find your good friends and keep them. Don't backstab anybody. Stick up for them. Stay real. You will carry that with you all through school, and you will have lifelong friends."

Environmentally Friendly

Here's a pop quiz, designed to give you a snapshot of how aware you are of the peer pressure in your everyday life.

True or False: There is an unspoken dress code at your school, which dictates what stores and what brands you ought to wear.

True or False: It's just a fact of life that people get picked on in middle school. It will pass; it's no big deal.

True or False: Most people in your school have figured out how they fit in to the social picture.

Kids who are bullied may grow up to bully others.

Answers

True. Every school has its own culture, and it usually includes a dress code even stricter than school uniforms.

True and False. It is a fact of life that people get picked on in middle school, but it's a very big deal. Victims of bullies can struggle with self-esteem and self-image well into adulthood, and their unexpressed anger can lead to some ugly situations.

Believe in Yourself

A recent study shows that adolescents who have confidence in their own ability to cope with bullies and pressure are less vulnerable to the negative effects. More than 2,000 students were asked how they dealt with aggressive attacks from others. Those who demonstrated good coping abilities didn't blame themselves, avoided aggressive behavior, and showed less social anxiety and depression than students who weren't as successful at defending themselves.

False. Some people are better at putting on a front than others, but just about all teens have the same anxieties and uncertainties and the feeling that everyone else got the *How to Be Cool* handbook.

How did you do? With a clear understanding of your environment, you can make smart choices about friends and influences.

Think With Your Whole Brain

Adolescence is the time when people develop greater cognitive skills. Kids in elementary school usually don't ponder what's happening to or around them, or think about why. Life just is. As you get older, though, the ability to analyze and figure things out also matures. This improved skill can be a huge help in navigating the wild and rocky terrain of the teen years. With

As you get older, your brain is able to handle more complex problems in subjects such as math and science and in your social life.

greater awareness comes greater self-assurance, which in turn can bolster self-esteem.

One psychologist noted, "The idea of self-esteem is the idea that we have a positive regard of ourselves based on how we perform and accomplish tasks such as school work or friendships. If we feel we're accepted, cool, then that adds to our sense of performing well and feeling safe. For many kids the definition of mental health is a good school, a safe home, and having someone to sit with in the lunchroom. Most kids don't have to be the most popular kid at school. They just want to do well."

A definite sense of self and an awareness of the world around you give you a strong foundation on which to build the Whole Authentic You. You really have to believe in it for it to work. You also need to recognize that only you can decide if you should do something—whether it's asking

someone out, taking a drag off someone else's cigarette, or making fun of the kid wearing silly shorts in gym class.

"There are too many followers," noted a school social worker. "My advice is to be a leader. Stick to your convictions, regardless. You'd rather have somebody like you for the true you than for whom you're trying to be."

Take the Garbage Out

Now the puzzle is coming together, and you've found the pieces that are your good friends. That won't make negative peer pressure magically disappear, but it can fortify your defenses against it. With a sense of your place in the world, it will be easier to interact with other classmates and peers without worrying about getting sucked into the dark side. You can watch the friendships and fights and melodramas unfold among

The Right Priorities

Stephanie has a strong sense of who she is. Although she's no stranger to peer pressure, she has so far managed to stay centered. Her refusal to skip school or fall in with the ruling crowd hasn't worked against her. "There's always a little voice in my mind saying go have a good time, but I have my priorities straight so it isn't too hard," she said. "I can make the right decisions and still be considered a cool girl. The only downside is feeling left out sometimes. Everyone has inside jokes, reminiscing about their moments, and you feel left out. I've made my peace with that."

There are many ways to be a leader.

your classmates without becoming a bit player in someone else's soap opera.

Meanwhile, fill your time with the friends and activities you enjoy, don't forget to study, and keep talking with your parents or other trusted adults who can help you work through problems. Be smart and avoid situations that will put you in the path of risky behavior, but always have an exit strategy in case you're taken by surprise.

You may find that your stand against negative peer pressure has become a model of peer influence and your friends are following your example. By refusing to be a follower, you may instead become a leader. Lead on!

QUIZ

How do you handle peer pressure and stay true to yourself? Take this quiz to find out!

1. The object of your affection occasionally makes snide comments about how you dress. You:
A) Dump the twit. You know you look awesome!
B) Put up with it. It's a small price to pay for being a couple.
C) Die of embarrassment and ask for advice on how to dress.

2. Some of your friends hassle you because you don't drink. You:
A) Ignore them. It's your choice, not theirs.
B) Fake an allergy to alcohol.
C) Drink around them to shut them up.

3. The popular group at school has been picking on the new kid. You:
A) Ask the poor soul to join you and your friends for lunch. After all, you were new once, too.
B) Don't interfere, but shoot the new kid a sympathetic look from across the room.
C) Stay out of it. You don't want the girls to turn on you next.

4. You get caught up in a moment and suddenly realize that what you're doing is wrong. Do you go through with it anyway?
A) No, never.
B) Once or twice. I'm only human.
C) Yes, often! I have trouble saying no.

5. Your friends urge you to lie to your parents to avoid getting in trouble. Do you do it?
A) Never. I can talk to my parents.
B) Occasionally, when it seems necessary.
C) Yep. Fairly often.

6. Have you ever done anything out of character, just to make somebody new like you?
A) No way! If they don't like me that's their problem.
B) Sometimes.
C) Of course! All the time!

If most of your answers were A, you are THE SUPERHERO:

Wow. You really know who you are and aren't afraid to stand up for yourself or for others. Keep your feet on the ground and your mind focused on what's important to you, and you'll be able to resist the worst peer pressure has to offer.

If most of your answers were B, you are THE POLITICIAN:

You like to choose your battles, which isn't a bad thing. However, working so hard to steer a safe course can make you a little too prone to doing what you think others want you to. Don't forget, we all have to live with the choices we make!

If most of your answers were C, you are THE PHANTOM:

Is anybody there? It's easy to persuade you or to push you around. As a result, your self-esteem can take a real beating, and it's tough to know who your real friends are. Dig deep for some inner strength and declare to the world who you are.

GLOSSARY

adolescence	period of life between puberty and adulthood
clique	small, exclusive group of friends
conform	act the same way as everyone else or in a way that's expected of you
norm	standard regarded as typical; an average
ostracized	excluded from a group
peer pressure	pressure from one's peers to behave in a manner similar or acceptable to them
psychology	science that deals with mental processes and behavior
self-esteem	pride in oneself; self-respect

WHERE TO GET HELP

Boys & Girls Clubs of America
1275 Peachtree St. N.E.
Atlanta, GA 30309-3506
404/487-5700
Boys & Girls Clubs of America operate clubs designed for youth programs and activities. Programs include leadership training, peer pressure resistance, and assertiveness training.

Camp Fire USA National Headquarters
1100 Walnut St., Suite 1900
Kansas City, MO 64106-2197
816/285-2010
Camp Fire is a coed, national organization that offers programs such as youth leadership, environmental education, and service learning. Youth meet in small groups and participate in a variety of activities, developing partnerships with adults as they build self-esteem and master skills that will benefit them throughout their lives.

Centers for Disease Control and Prevention
1600 Clifton Road
Atlanta, GA 30333
800/311-3435
The CDC has many resources to help adolescents make smart choices in their lives. The CDC hosts a teen-oriented Web site, www.bam.gov, that has a lot of great information.

4-H
1400 Independence Ave. S.W.
Washington, D.C. 20250-2225
202/720-2908
4-H involves millions of young people in programs promoting personal responsibility, leadership, and life skills. 4-H programs encompass many areas of interest, including photography, conservation, science, and technology.

National Institute on Alcohol Abuse & Alcoholism
5635 Fishers Lane, MSC 9304
Bethesda, MD 20892-9304
301/443-3860
The NIAAA provides information about alcohol abuse prevention. It has a terrific Web site for teens that deals specifically with alcohol and peer pressure, www. thecoolspot.gov.

National Mental Health Information Center
P.O. Box 42557
Washington, DC 20015
800/789-2647
This organization is a division of the U.S. Department of Health and Human Services. It offers information and help for people with questions about mental health.

YMCA of the USA
101 N. Wacker Drive
Chicago, IL 60606
800/872-9622 or 888/333-9622
YMCAs offer safe environments for young people and dedicated adults who listen to them and help them with the problems that come with adolescence. Special programs for teens and preteens focus on relationship-building and development of the inner strength to avoid destructive behavior. Each YMCA operates independently. Call the number above to find your local branch.

45

SOURCE NOTES

Chapter 1
Page 4, line 17: Stephanie. Orange County, Calif. Telephone interview. 12 June 2008.
Page 6, column 1, line 2: Jean Cosgrave. Plainfield, Ill. Personal interview. 18 June 2008.
Page 6, column 2, line 2: Erin. Braintree, Mass. Personal interview. 29 June 2008.
Page 6, sidebar, lines 3 and 9: Mike. Naperville, Ill. Personal interview. 5 June 2008.
Page 8, sidebar, line 8: Ibid.
Page 8, sidebar, line 16: Elise. Oak Park, Ill. Telephone interview. 28 June 2008.
Page 8, sidebar, line 25: Rob. Minneapolis, Minn. E-mail interview. 24 June 2008.
Page 8, sidebar, line 31: Erin.
Page 9, column 1, line 7: Lauren. Forest Lake, Minn. E-mail interview. 19 June 2008.
Page 9, column 2, line 3. Ibid.

Chapter 2
Page 12, column 2, line 8: Marc Atkins. University of Illinois, Chicago. Telephone interview. 18 June 2008.
Page 14, column 1, line 18: Stephanie.
Page 14, column 2, line 1: Julia. Elburn, Ill. Telephone interview. 29 July 2008.
Page 14, column 2, lines 15 and 25: Elise.
Page 15, sidebar, lines 3, 7, and 13: Julia.
Page 18, column 1, lines 18 and 23: Erin.

Chapter 3
Page 20, column 1, line 3: Atkins.
Page 20, column 1, line 21: Rob.
Page 20, column 2, line 6: Lisa Barney. Lisle, Ill. Personal interview. 24 June 2008.
Page 20, column 2, line 24: Atkins.
Page 21, sidebar, lines 12 and 23: Rob.
Page 22, column 1, line 4: Erin.
Page 22, column 2, line 5: Barney.
Page 22, column 2, line 16: Elise.

Page 24, sidebar, lines 5 and 14: Lauren.
Page 25, column 2, line 12: Stephanie.
Page 26, column 1, lines 5 and 24: Julia.
Page 27, column 1, line 14: Erin.

Chapter 4
Page 31, column 1, line 24: Barney.
Page 32, column 1, line 5: Stephanie.
Page 32, sidebar, lines 5 and 16: Erin.
Page 32, column 2, line 14: Cosgrave.
Page 32, column 2, line 21: Mike.
Page 33, column 2, line 6: Atkins.
Page 34, sidebar, lines 4 and 7: Elise.
Page 34, column 1, line 3: Julia.
Page 34, column 1, line 12: Rob.
Page 34, column 2, line 13: Ibid.
Page 35, column 2, line 6: Lauren.

Chapter 5
Page 38, sidebar, line 1: Rob.
Page 38, sidebar, line 5: Elise.
Page 38, sidebar, line 8: Lauren.
Page 38, sidebar, line 12: Stephanie.
Page 38, sidebar, line 17: Mike.
Page 38, sidebar, line 20: Julia.
Page 38, sidebar, line 28: Erin.
Page 41, column 1, line 4: Atkins.
Page 41, column 2, line 5: Cosgrave.
Page 42, sidebar, line 8, Stephanie.

Fiction

Blume, Judy. *Blubber.* New York: Dell Yearling, 1986.

Clugston, Chynna. *Queen Bee.* New York: Scholastic Graphix, 2005.

Cormier, Robert. *The Chocolate War.* New York: Knopf Books for Young Readers, 1986.

Hinton, S.E. *The Outsiders.* New York: Viking Press, 1967.

Holmes, Elisabeth. *Pretty Is.* New York: Dutton Juvenile, 2007.

Spinelli, Jerry. *Stargirl.* New York: Knopf Books for Young Readers, 2002.

Walter, Eric. *House Party.* Orca Soundings: Victoria, B.C.: Orca Book Publishers, 2007.

Nonfiction

Cherniss, Hilary, and Sara Jane Sluke. *Complete Idiot's Guide to Surviving Peer Pressure for Teens.* New York: Alpha Books, 2002.

Erlbach, Arlene. *The Middle School Survival Guide.* New York: Walker & Company, 2003.

Shearin Karres, Erika V. *Mean Chicks, Cliques and Dirty Tricks.* Cincinnati: Adams Media, 2004.

Stewart, Gail B. *Peer Pressure.* Farmington Hills, Mich.: KidHaven Press, 2003.

Wiseman, Rosalind. *Queen Bees and Wannabes.* New York: Random House, 2002.

For more information on this topic, use FactHound.

1. Go to *www.facthound.com*

2. Choose your grade level.

3. Begin your search.

This book's ID number is 9780756518912

FactHound will find the best sites for you.

INDEX

ABOUT THE AUTHOR

Amy Rechner is the author of several nonfiction books for children and adults and has written extensively on education and safety issues. Rechner lives in the Chicago area with her husband and daughter.

ABOUT THE CONTENT ADVISER

Billy AraJeJe Woods has a doctorate in psychology, a master's in education, and a bachelor's in psychology. He has been counseling individuals and families for more than 25 years. He is a certified transactional analysis counselor and a drug and alcohol abuse counselor. A professor of psychology at Saddleback College, Mission Viejo, California, Woods teaches potential counselors to work with dysfunctional families and special populations. He began his counseling career in the military, where he worked with men and women suffering from post-traumatic stress disorder. In his practice, Woods has worked with many young adults on issues related to drug and alcohol abuse and body image.